Israel, the Nations and the Future?

A TV script based on Biblical Principles

By **Dr Jay Rawlings**

Copyright © 2015 Jerusalem Vistas - Israel Vision
All rights reserved. Written permission must be secured from the authors to use or reproduce any part of this book.

Scripture quotations from New King James Version, copyright 1982 Thomas Nelson. Used by permission. All rights reserved.

ISBN 978-965-7542-36-1

Photos by C. Stephan, J. Rawlings and Reynold Mainse

Cover photo: Massada, Israel

This publication is made possible through the kind support of Friends of Jerusalem Vistas and Israel Vision

Lectures - Power Points

If you would like Jay and/or Meridel to visit your area to speak on, Timeless Secrets, Bible Prophesy, **Israel, the Bible and the Future,** Christian Zionism, Healing for the Family, or other related topics, see the information below,

Order information:

Jerusalem Vistas/Israel Vision
P O Box 84156
Mevasseret Zion 9079097
Israel

Email: jvistas@gmail.com or jvrawlings@gmail.com

www.israelvisiontv.blogspot.com

CONTENTS

Part 1 - Introduction 5

Part 2 - Sheep and Goat Nations 13

Part 3 - Historic Panorama of the Nations 22

Part 4 - World Systems 37

Part 5 - Democracy Today 41

Part 6 - Islam-ocracy 45

Part 7 - Theocracy 49

Part 8 - Kingdom of God on Earth 53

Part 9 - Prayer - the Greatest Power of All 55

Part 10 - Your Part 59

       About the Speakers/Authors 61

       Contact information 62

       Production Stills 63

INTRODUCTION

- **Ancient and modern nations - ancient spirits - today**
- ***"Israel, Iran and the Bible"*** **- prince of Persia spirit - kill the Jews then. NOW destroy Israel; Muslim false messiah, see Ezekiel 38**
- **"Israel, Syria and the Bible" - Assyrian spirit - disperse the Jews then - NOW destroy Israel; Terror + Shi'ites. Ezekiel 32; Isaiah 17:1**
- **Ephesians 6:12 -** *"We wrestle not against flesh and blood but against principalities, against powers, against the rulers of the darkness of this age, against spiritual hosts of wickedness in heavenly places. Therefore take up the whole armour of God."*

[Title and Slide # 1 and cut to Jay - location Mount of Olives, Jerusalem
Note: Each slide appears in the DVD at the appropriate time]

Israel, the Nations and the Future

Part 1

Introduction

Shalom from the Mount of Olives! I just love this panoramic view of Jerusalem, its Old City walls, the Temple Mount and the Golden Gate known in Hebrew as the "Mercy Gate". One day the Messiah will enter Jerusalem through this gate and set up His everlasting government of loving-kindness, peace, righteousness and equity for all people and all nations on earth.

What a day that will be! In fact most people on earth long for such a time of relief and tranquility.
But before that happens, there are important events that must take place right here. That is our topic today. It concerns current events and near future happenings in the light of Scripture. Understanding this plan with discernment will give true "seekers" in every nation comfort and confidence when facing the future. Perhaps that is you?

Israel, the Nations and the Future

This presentation is part three of my series of DVD's, entitled, **"Israel, Iran and the Bible," "Israel, Syria and the Bible", and now "Israel, the Nations and the Future."** Yes, the future is a mystery. But as we look back in time we can actually see the future... How? This can be done by studying the Bible in the context of human history.

The Word of God is actually "His Story" played out through the history of mankind. Curiously, at about midway in the present time line of the nations, the Psalmist asks,
"Why do the nations rage and imagine a vain thing?"
Later while speaking here on the Mount of Olives **Jesus** *pointed to a time when* **"men's hearts will fail them for fear!"** *Psalm 2:1; Luke 21:26*

This perfectly describes conditions on earth **TODAY.** Nations raging against each other, chaos, civil wars, international unrest, terror, violence, hunger, starvation, abuses of all kinds, brother against brother, and horrific suffering that is occurring all around the globe as we speak. It is a scary time indeed.

THE FEAR FACTOR

[location Ben Yehuda walking mall - Jerusalem]

People are afraid. They want to know, "What is going to happen next...? What will happen, "to me, my family, my city and my country" ? Truly we are living in frightening days. The world economy is near collapse. Terror and violence fill the earth, especially the Middle East. Warfare on innocent civilians causing horrific human suffering is out of control. Peace negotiators, the world over, keep coming up empty handed time after time! It seems the words of the weeping Hebrew prophet Jeremiah are more relevant now than ever before,
> *"Peace, peace and there is no peace...we searched for a time of peace but no good came, and for a time of healing but all we got was trouble and war!"*
Jeremiah 8:11,15

[cut to new location Jerusalem's Independence Park - holding up a newspaper]

Nearly every newspaper in the world today has a horoscope column. Why?
Because from ancient times, instead of turning to the **"Master Designer"** of the universe, people have always looked elsewhere to get 'hints' about the future. Fortune tellers and astrologers have always been eager and available substitutes. With such human "forecasts", one is supposedly told how to act on what is coming. But these man-made predictions are only wisps of smoke that evaporate with time.

The only authoritative source concerning the future is the Word of God. The Bible contains the story of Israel intertwined with other nations. Starting with one man and one woman, they became a family, then clans, next tribes and eventually a nation. Yes, Israel evolved into a new, yet old nation state, which is a modern and free democracy.

This panorama takes over 5,000 years. All of which leads up to the ultimate government on earth for all nations. That is, of course, the rule of the Messiah of Israel from Jerusalem. His government of brotherhood, loving equity, moral justice and righteousness brings peace to everyone on board planet Earth. **EVERYONE!!!** This is the only hope that will provide exactly what all people, in every nation are so desperately fighting and struggling to attain! Lasting PEACE!

Signs of the Times

- **Opinion Poll - "What kind of TV shows do you want to see? Answer:** *"We want to know what is going go happen in the future. We are afraid!"*
- **Disciples asked Jesus: "When - What - How?"**
- **Answered in Matthew 24 and 25, Mark 13, Luke 21 - insider information**
- **Look for Physical signs/Spiritual Signs - insider information**
- **Israel = Physical & Spiritual signs <u>together</u>**
- **"Be alert, let no one deceive you + Watch & PRAY!"**

SIGNS OF THE TIMES

[title + slide # 3 on screen - location on Mt of Olives - Jerusalem]

In the First Century, Jesus shocked his disciples by predicting the destruction of the Temple in Jerusalem. Was He talking about their beloved Temple? To them, this just didn't make any sense. So, to get clarification, they came to Him privately here on the Mount of Olives asking;
When will these things be?
What will be the sign of your coming?...and
What will usher in the end of this age?

Jesus, then gave them **"insider information"**. HE TOLD THEM THE HARD TRUE FACTS and yet at the same time gave them the keys to understand His difficult words. First He warned, as recorded in Matt 24:4;
   "Be Alert - Don't be deceived and beware that no one tricks you". Over and over He said, **"Watch and Pray"**.

Then he explained the signs to look for at the end of this age. First, He described the,
- **physical signs**, next the,
- **spiritual signs**, which we can discern happening on earth today. Then thirdly,
- a **mixture of spiritual and physical signs**. The spiritual and physical combine in Jerusalem, with the Jewish people, and the nation of Israel. This is quite a mystery.

In my previous teachings on this topic, I discussed many of these signs in detail, all of which are coming to pass, right in front of our eyes.

Here is a short list of what He said to look out for:

1. False messiah's
2. Wars and rumors of war
3. Nation rising against nation
4. Kingdom against kingdom
5. Famines, flooding, global warming, and pre-occupation with weather
6. Diseases
7. Earthquakes with resultant tsunami's and "super storms"
8. Hatred and intolerance against believers in God
9. Betrayals and intrigues
10. Lawlessness - violence, killing, terror, abuses and starvations.
11. The love of one's neighbor for others, vanishing on a wide scale.
12. Then the final sign he mentioned, is that all countries will be divided into either **"Sheep or Goat" nations** based on certain criteria which we will discuss shortly.

A recent opinion poll was conducted in the United States where the question asked randomly to people on the street was, "What type of TV show are you interested in seeing"?
The majority of respondents of various ages, genders and professions said, "We want to see TV programs that are going to tell us what is going to happen in the future, because we are afraid"!

But in spite of all of these worrisome signs, He said, to **"look up"** and "not to give up" but **"to endure"** to the end. Why? Because, the *"**Good News" of the Kingdom of God* will be announced to ALL NATIONS...*then and only then* will the end come! Matthew 24:14

Now in **Part 2** of this presentation, lets examine some more interesting details about the future of your nation.
Can you make a difference in the eternal destiny of your country? I believe you can.

Stay tuned to find out how!

Photos: www.reynoldmainse - used with permission

Is the Eternal Destiny of Nations Being set Today?

- Matthew 25:31-40 "Sheep and Goat" nations
- Mercy = Moral character + social action
- National attitudes to the "least of My brethren"
- Treatment of Jews & Nation of Israel - 1948
- Genesis 12:3 - God's eternal principles

Israel, the Nations and the Future

Part 2

SHEEP AND GOAT NATIONS

Is the Eternal Destiny of Nations being set Today?

[slide #4 on screen - location Nebi Musa in the Judean Desert]

The last end time sign that Jesus mentioned in his private message to His disciples on the Mount of Olives was more like a prophecy concerning the future and judgement of the nations. For details please see Matthew 25: 31-40

Jesus, in this discussion, does not call Himself the "Messiah" nor the 'King" but refers in this prophecy to the **"Son of Man"... coming in His glory with His holy angels with Him",** just as the prophet Daniel before Him did. He goes on to say that, **then, the King will sit on the throne of His glory while all the nations will be gathered before Him, and He will separate them as a shepherd divides his sheep from the goats.** This separation, to the right hand meaning *blessed*, are the sheep, while the goats go to the left. The separation is a severe division; based on showing "mercy" to those in need. He describes the needy as, **the poor, the hungry and thirsty, the sick, those in prison and those needing clothing.** This means that the return of the Messiah will usher in a judgement that will divide people groups and nations based upon their acts of charity to those He called, **"the least of these My brethren".**

Simply said, the division of the sheep from the goats will be based on national character and this character is revealed by social actions of moral justice or the lack of them.
So, outward evidence of moral character demonstrates inner righteousness or unrighteousness.

As someone said, *"good works do not produce good character, good character produces good works".* So, Jesus very clearly teaches that national evidence of acts of moral character can be a determining factor concerning the eternal destinies of peoples groups or nations.
Those that qualify, He calls **"sheep nations."**

I like to think of such status as being based on national choices. Those countries whose citizens vote for leaders whose national policies involve giving charity to those in need have a better chance of being recognized as **"sheep nations"** than those who do not. Then **goat nations** have leaders who enslave their populations, refusing to call for such national acts of charity and who aggressively oppress other nations. They will be judged accordingly. Thankfully, there is a God of Justice.

Jesus personalizes this sign when He says,
> ***"If you do this to one of the least of these My brethren you do it to Me".*** Matthew 25:40b

Now, we know that anyone in need is indeed **"one of His brethren"**. But on the other hand Jesus' *natural* brethren were and are the Jewish people. That fact can never be altered. Please never forget that the early Christians were mainly Jews and they are responsible for taking the 'good news' out from Jerusalem to the Gentile nations. Nowhere in scripture does it say the Church has replaced the Jewish people as many believe and teach. Beware of subtle doctrines of anti-Semitism, be they against Jew or Arab. Both peoples are beloved of God, as are all peoples on earth.

> Genesis 12: 3 teaches: ***"I will bless them who bless you (the seed of Abraham) and curse him who curses you."***

It is clear that, national 'attitudes' towards Jews and Israel, can be a deciding factor for blessing or cursing. Consider this for a moment. What is the criteria for my country to receive the status of a *"sheep or goat"* nation? This is a very sobering thought. Of course these are my opinions.

HOW NATIONS TREAT THE NATION OF ISRAEL

It is written:
"The land which I gave Abraham and Isaac I give to you (Jacob); and to your descendants after you I give this land." Genesis 35:12

One other factor connected to this prophecy that I think must also be considered is **how nations treat the nation of Israel. To me this is a crucial and deciding issue whether they will be sheep or goat nations.** This has had current relevance since 1948 when Israel became a nation. The point is very clear because God's Word in the book of Joel gives two criteria for national judgements based on,

1.   Did they, in the past, drive the Jews out of the holy land? And
2.   Today, do they push for the division of the land that God calls, "My land?"

Historic anti-Semitism was against the Jewish people. Today neo anti-Semitism is focused **against the nation of Israel**. If you want proof of this just keep reading!

"I will gather all nations, and bring them down to the Valley of Jehoshaphat; and I will enter into judgement with them there on account of My people, My heritage Israel, whom they have scattered among the nations; they have also divided up My land" Joel 3:2

A TWO STATE SOLUTION

So, according to Scripture, the continual call by world leaders to divide the Holy land into **"two states"** is actually a prescription for Divine judgement. Everyone thinks it will solve the Middle East crisis between Israel and the Palestinians.
Actually, the nations are blind to the consequences of this widely held position. Nearly every "expert" on earth today calls for a **"two state solution,"** one Palestinian and one Israeli.

This sounds very plausible but there are two main problems in taking this position. **First, it does not have a Biblical basis and secondly, every time Israel, in good faith, has "given up land for peace", it has never produced peace but has actually, created war.**

Why?
Because when Israel retreats and gives up land, to the Moslem mind, this is perceived as weakness, and it means that Allah has triumphed over the "infidel" Jews. The Muslims do not see it as a genuine gesture toward peace and reconciliation, but Israel's longing for peace and will to make concessions, confirms to them the idea that one day they will get **all the lands** (nations) of the infidels worldwide.

Why?
According to their Islamic doctrine they must rule over the lesser **"dhimmi's** forever. Non Muslims are called "dhimmi's" in Arabic, especially Jews and Christians. What does this mean in real terms?

ISRAELI WITHDRAWAL = PEACE? YES OR NO?

For example when Israel withdrew from south Lebanon in 2000, Haifa, Acco and Nahariya were immediately hit with thousands of deadly rockets fired by Hezbollah terrorists from the vacated land. It is vital to note that this Israeli withdrawal was in compliance with UN resolution 425.

Next, in 2006 when Israel withdrew 8000 Israeli citizens from their community of Gaza called Gush Kattif to placate world opinion, the Hamas terrorists immediately moved into their vacated modern homes and prosperous farms. They destroyed them and turned the area into rocket launching pads.

Since then these terrorists have fired more than 10,000 rockets against Israeli civilians in urban centers such as Ashkelon, Ashdod, Sderot and Beer Sheva, holding about 1 million Israeli's virtual hostages in that area.

Meanwhile the world community continues to criticize Israel as being the "aggressor" and continues to call for Israel to give up **more** "land for peace." Today its the so-called *West Bank,* which is actually the Jewish heartland of Judea and Samaria. I ask you, "will this bring lasting peace? No, because what they really want is **all** of the land of Israel. According to Islamic doctrine "infidels" cannot have it. Here is what the Word says;

> *"They have said, 'Come and let us cut them off from being a nation that the name of Israel be remembered no more.* Psalm 83:4

ISRAEL SURROUNDED BY ENEMIES

The Iranian terror regime, with its capital in Teheran, have successfully surrounded Israel by their surrogate terrorists. For example, in the north, by Hezbollah based in Lebanon, while in the south, by Hamas in Gaza. Trouble continues on the eastern border by President Assad's Shiite army. Iran has armed all of these groups with 100,000's of deadly rockets. They are all pointed at Israel.

Some rockets supplied by Russia and China have been intercepted and destroyed en route to Lebanon from Iran while on the ground in Syria. This was accomplished by Israeli air strikes. Prime Minister Benjamin Netanyahu has declared that "such long range deadly accurate weapons will never reach the hands of terrorists like Hezbullah".

Just recently we filmed the arrival of the *Klos - C* freighter, escorted to the Port of Eilat by the Israeli navy. Its hold was filled with deadly long range M 302 missles headed for Gaza.

Israel traced their circuitous route from China to Damascus, where the missiles were enhanced, then taken overland to Iran, and secretly loaded onto a Panamanian ship headed for Port Sudan. There they were to be taken across Africa to Egypt and smuggled into Gaza.

Thank God, Israel routinely stops such ships.

"No weapon formed against you shall prosper. And every tongue that rises against you in judgment You shall condemn. This is the heritage of the servants of the LORD, and their righteousness is from Me, says the LORD." Isaiah 54:17

THE THREE "NO'S"

This conflict goes one step further with Israel's enemies viciously attacking **the right of Israel to exist** among the family of nations. This is audacious and pugnacious. Their propaganda and untruths grow more out of proportion with each passing day. This strategy is not new. Of the 193 nations registered with the United Nations today, the majority of Muslim states will not recognize the right of Israel to exist. The basis for this position was birthed in August 1967 when the *Arab League* met in Khartoum, following their defeat by Israel in the 1967 *Six Day War*. To this day these enemies of Israel cannot cede victory to Israel. We were in Egypt recently, and they were celebrating their "victory in the 1967 War". This sickness of hatred grows and grows.

The deceptive spirit overshadowing the Khartoum Conference, 47 years ago, inspired the Arab nations to proudly draw the following conclusions concerning Israel:
  "No negotiation; No recognition and No peace."

Again, this 'non recognition' position could not have been taken until Israel became a nation in 1948. Since then, Israel is expected by the world community to make peace with those who refuse to acknowledge her right to exist. In the current "peace talks" Prime Minister Netanyahu has repeatedly called for the Palestinian negotiators to at least recognize Israel's existence as a starting point. So far this has not happened. Israel continues to be blamed for the breakdown in the 'peace process'. Nabil Shaath, veteran Palestinian negotiator says. "We will never recognize the Zionist entity!

How many nations in the world today would put up with such nonsense if they were in Israel's position? **NONE.** The situation would be humorous if it wasn't so tragic.

Now back to the **"Sheep and Goat** prophecy of Jesus. Remember this was the last end time prophecy He gave.
It seems to me that this "sign" of how to determine the destiny of a whole country is a mystery. Yet it is clearly connected to the posture of the hearts of the righteous people in every nation whether leaders or not. What am I getting at?

Well, according to the Bible there is the precedent of "saving a people" based on a certain number of righteous people living in that nation or city state. This happened when Abraham pleaded with God to save Sodom and Gomorrah. God said to him, ***"If you can find ten righteous people in Sodom I will save it".*** See Genesis 18:32 for the details. Interestingly that is why today in any Jewish synagogue or prayer gathering there must be a quorum, or "*minyan*" in Hebrew, of at least 10 men before they can begin their prayers.

Now... let's move ahead to about 600 BCE to one of the most pivotal dreams in the history of mankind.

A DREAM AND A VISION

[Title on screen - location Nebi Musa, Judean Desert, Israel]

Other than Jesus' words the most accurate sign of all, concerning the future, has to do with King Nebuchadnezzer's dream and it's interpretation. The dream was given to one of the most powerful potentates of all time. He was the founder of the Neo-Babylonian Empire that later spawned the Medo Persian Empire. He was an absolute monarch whose word and wish was law. But, he was troubled by something that he couldn't "get". It was a dream that gave him a double problem! He could not remember the dream, nor grasp its meaning. So he called together all of the astrologers, fortune tellers, magicians, palm readers and soothsayers of his empire and ordered them to not only tell him the forgotten dream, but also its interpretation. They were then told that if they could not reveal to him the dream and its interpretation they would **all** be killed.

None could get it! The schedule was set. The day of their execution loomed. They were all about to be slaughtered one by one... until a solitary man, saved their lives. He was one of the Hebrew young men, taken captive in Jerusalem and brought bound to Babylon along with all Jews who became slaves. The scripture says: **"God gave them knowledge and skill in all literature and wisdom and Daniel had understanding in all visions and dreams."** Jesus called him **'the prophet'** and said, **"whom ever reads what he says let him understand!"** See Matt 24:15. It was not a request, it was written in the imperative verb form. It was/is an order.

Stay with me to find out who **is** this mystery man! How did he "save the day"? In Part 4 you will discover the exciting details. But before that we are now going to look back through the annals of history, over thousands of years to discover how man has tried to rule and govern himself, sometimes successfully but mostly WITHOUT SUCCESS!

Israel, the Nations and the Future

Part 3

HISTORIC PANORAMA OF THE NATIONS

Systems of Human Governance from Antiquity

[location - Jaffa lookout with a panorama view of the Tel Aviv skyline and beaches]

The brilliant, world renowned, British astronomer and scientist, Stephen Hawking, declared concerning the mystery of man's beginnings; *"You cannot understand the glories of the Universe without believing there is some Supreme Power behind it".* A Brief History of Time, 1988.

Then, Hugh Ross, a Canadian contemporary of Hawking's goes on to say, *" A Creator must exist. The 'Big Bang' ripples are clearly pointing to an* ex nihilo *or 'out of nothing' creation consistent with the first few verses of the book of Genesis.* The Fingerprint of God, pp 181-2.

Such remarks by two of the world's most revered and respected theoretical physicists since Albert Einstein, begs the obvious first question, "who initiated the "Big Bang?" Secondly these statements affirm the clear relevance of the Bible to the history of the development of our universe, planet and mankind.

The topic of Creation is definitely for another study but suffice it to say that the Biblical narrative gives valuable clues to the early stages of man's development as a social creature on earth. The first verse of the Bible describes *"the creation of the heavens and the earth"* while curiously the second verse gives a description of *"darkness and chaos".*

What happened, and for how long? No one knows! Next, however, in verse 3 of Genesis chapter 1, God commands that *"order be brought out of the chaos"*. How?
Simply, by bringing forth **"Light"**.

LIGHT OUT OF DARKNESS

Hence the luminary bodies, the sun, moon and stars are brought forth. Then the Creator moves into high gear bringing to life the plant kingdom, followed by the great sea creatures and finally He completes the formation of the animal kingdom on earth. Thus, surveying His creation He says that "what He has done... "*is "good"!*

Now wait. There is something missing. So just before the Sabbath or "day of rest" the Creator, ponders and says, *"Let us make man in Our image, according to Our likeness.* These verses introduce a phrase that is the cornerstone of the understanding of man. He was created *"in the image of God!" This happened when, "God formed man from the dust of the ground and breathed into his nostrils the breath of life and man became a living being"...with a "free will"* see Genesis 2:7 Then He declares that what He has done is... *"very good!"*

Thus, **"the image of God"** is presented first and foremost in relation to something absolutely new and original... **a family.** It is a divinely inspired, unique social order or community concept of God's character... in action. He creates mankind as male and female, not as solitary individuals, but two people, **Adam and Eve**, who were to become *one* in the marriage bond. Thus He created *THE FAMILY UNIT!*

So from time immemorial the family is the basic "building block" of all future social order and this is as true today as it was at the dawn of human history.

SOCIAL ORDER ON EARTH

[location - Jaffa lookout over Tel Aviv skyline and beaches]

We know from the biblical panorama of man's journey on earth that it has not been a smooth ride. Families and people groups derived from Adam lived long during the first 10 generations of the pre-Flood period. Then the degeneration of the human race proceeded rapidly in spite of a few Godly men such as, Enoch and Noah. The situation then, I think, was much like today with the world filled with **"corruption, violence and lawlessness."** Genesis 6:11. One of the Bible's recurring themes is that some 'intervention' has to be made in order to save man from his plunge into degradation and self destruction. It lays bare the absolute need for his redemption and restoration.

> ***"Then the Lord saw that the wickedness of man was great in the earth, and that every intent of the thoughts of his heart were only evil continually.***
> ***"And the Lord was sorry that he had made man on the earth, and that He was grieved in His heart...saying 'I will destroy man whom I have created from the face of the earth...But Noah found grace in the eyes of the Lord."*** Genesis 6: 5,6,7a, 8

After the Flood the Lord promised Noah and his family of 8 souls that He would never destroy humankind ever again by a flood and confirmed this covenant by the "sign of the rainbow." Then the sons of Noah, Shem, Ham and Japheth went out from the Ark and *"from these the whole earth was populated."* Genesis 9:19

A list of the nations derived from these three men is found in Genesis 10. Sadly, their descendants quickly reverted to pagan ways so the Lord decided to confuse their language at the *Tower of Babel* and then He scattered them all over the face of the earth.

So what they intended as a monument to human effort became a symbol of divine judgement against human pride and self-rule. But all was not lost. God had another plan waiting to be implemented and that involved, **"The Hebrew People."**

THE HEBREWS

[title on screen - location - overlooking the Western Wall, Jerusalem]

The Hebrews laid the foundation for a different social order containing a divine plan. The whole purpose of the Hebrews was to introduce to mankind the way to have a personal relationship with the Creator. Through Biblical Israel, Father God set in motion the pattern of compassionate righteousness & moral justice. Hebrew prophets and scribes were chosen to pen the thoughts and Words of the Almighty. Consequently, the Bible is a living legacy for all peoples and all **nations** on earth.

Abram, later called Abraham *'the father of many nations'* received a sovereign call, *to get out and leave his birthplace of idol worshippers and to go to a land that he did not know. It was a great test of faith!* His positive response formed the pivotal moment that led to the development of his family, which later became 'the Patriarchs'. They grew to be 12 tribes, and birthed the nation of Israel at Mount Sinai. They were promised the Land of Israel, to be ruled by the entire Davidic line including the Messiah. This ancient nation is the only one to survive to modern time.

So Genesis 12:1-3 reveals Abrams obedience to the call of the Almighty. Yes, he went to... ***"this land...that I will show you!"*** His obedience created the very basis for the principle of "blessing" as opposed to "cursing". Pay close attention to the fierce struggle, still growing in the earth 4,000 years removed from Abraham.

This truth is a universal, everlasting principle of compassionate righteousness and moral justice set in motion by the Lord God Himself. If you read Genesis 17: 5-8 the Abrahamic Covenant was given by God. The recipients were specifically stated as, "Abraham and his descendants through Isaac" promising that they would be "**His people**"... **forever.** At the same time they were also given **"the Land of Promise"... forever.** These two unbreakable covenant promises form the foundation for all the other thousands of covenantal promises found in the Bible. Some would say that that "it is the 'mother' of all the 1000's of covenant/promises given by God to man.

Isaac's wife Rebecca felt the physical struggle of twins in her womb. She sought God for answers, He gave insight. ***"Two nations are in your womb, Two peoples shall be separated from your body; One people shall be stronger than the other, and the older shall serve the younger."*** Genesis 25:23

No, we do not understand this. From the womb, Jacob was chosen to walk one road, and Esau chose the opposite. He despised his birthright, sold it to Jacob, and left his family to move in with another family, the clans of Ishmael. This unexpected sequence of events makes us wonder why God chooses as He does? He works in the lives of an obedient people to counter the effects of the disobedient. God's plan from the dawn of history has been for the redemption of **all mankind**.

He created a nation and people whom He would use to bring blessing to **all** families upon earth. The conditions are simple. Any individual and/or nation who blesses Abraham's descendants through Isaac are blessed by God. Those who persecute them are cursed by God. (past, present and future).
Herein lies yet another mystery.

NATIONAL BLESSING VERSUS NATIONAL CURSING

[Title on screen - location Western wall Jerusalem]

Today we are all aware of the unrest among the nations. Some say this is the result of God's judgement. On the other hand, I say that what we see today is the outward workings or result of God's correction of the nations. Why? Because most nations have "cursed" Israel as a nation. For decades, in some cases centuries or even millennia hatred of the Jews and their Biblical cause and nation is repeated.

Thus the root cause of the horrific scenes happening among the nations today is God's principle of *"what you sow you will reap."* Tragically MOST MUSLIM nations and many other non-aligned nations have denied the Jewish people and their nation, Israel, **the right to exist.** Actually all nations around the world (with few exceptions) are calling for a dividing up of the Holy Land. Jerusalem is the prize that in folly, "empires have sought to own", and as a result have been reduced to ashes. This toxic and tragic attitude is evident since 1947 among the nations. National opinions and political policies regarding Israel are recorded for all to see, in their UN voting records and via the wars started against the "Zionist entity".

Of all of the resolutions made in the UN countering any nation, note that an amazing **85% are against Israel.** Why? Especially when in fact, Israel is the only real democracy in the Middle East? The UN exonerates countries like North Korea which carries a 52 year old history of slave labor camps on the level of Auschwitz? It is simply past human understanding. Let's discuss "human-rights", involving women and girls in Saudi Arabia and Iran? Yet, both of these nations are in good standing in the UN and serve on the Human Rights committee!

From the birth of the UN, Israel was at a disadvantage. Muslim and Arab member states out numbered democracies so they had the voting edge. Israel suffered isolation due to oil rich nations threatening Israel's allies with embargoes. Arab, Muslim and Third World non-aligned nations united into a powerful voting bloc with a powerful majority of 124 to 69. Their goal was to discredit the US and delegitimize Israel. **Today they have the power to pass a resolution saying that** *"the earth is flat and that Israel flattened it."*. They have placed Israel on its permanent *Human Rights Agenda.* Israel which has equal rights for all of its citizens, minority rights, civil liberties, and a growing population of Jews, Christians and Muslims! The Honorable Danny Ayalon who served as Israel's Ambassador to the UN from 1993 to 1997 says, *"I saw first hand the hypocrisy, the cynicism of the* **political interests** *that have taken over the United Nations. I have watched dictators applauded, murder, and terrorism ignored and human rights turned into a travesty."*

Thus, ironically the State of Israel is the watershed nation that will eventually determine the final status of each nation. This is according to the last sign Jesus said to look for before He returns to rule in equity. What a chilling word.

Repeat after me:
"My nation is going to be judged before the Lord God of Israel, based on how they (we) treated the Jews and national Israel."

In my opinion we must take very seriously those people called by Jesus, *"the least of these my brethren"*.

WHEN DID ISRAEL BECOME A NATION?

[Location- Knesset Menorah monument -
near Israel's Parliament, Jerusalem]

It is important to remember that Israel only became a **nation** after their 'Exodus' and miraculous deliverance from Egyptian slavery under Moses leadership. Prior to that they were families and clans or tribes eventually known by the names of their forefathers, the 12 sons of Jacob. Until their 430 year sojourn in Egypt, they were an agricultural group of people and later slaves whose principal patriarch was Abraham, who traced his lineage through his sons Isaac and Jacob. Jacob's name meaning "supplanter" was later changed to "Israel", a "prince with God". Then he returned to Israel the land promised to his grandfather Abraham.

Joseph, one of the sons of Jacob was sold into slavery in Egypt and became the most powerful man in that land because of the blessing of wisdom he had received from God. **His interpretation of Pharaoh's dream** gave him the plan to save up food during the "times of plenty" which actually preserved the Egyptian nation during "times of famine," while simultaneously saving his own family even though he was unrecognizable to them. As the 'Vizier' or the Second in Command of Egypt he looked like an Egyptian. During his days on earth Joseph's life parallels the life of Jesus in more than 60 ways. His secret revelation of himself to his family is a foreshadowing of the revelation of the Messiah to national Israel as recorded in Zechariah 12:10.

Now lets consider the reason why the Hebrew people are the only ancient people on the globe today who are flourishing in their original God given land, speaking their original Biblical language of Hebrew and worshipping the God of their fathers. Today they are known as Israeli's. What has held them together against all odds? I believe the honor given to the family unity is a secret, including the command to 'honor' one's parents.

This tradition or commandment is practiced faithfully by keeping the Sabbath.

"Therefore the children of Israel shall keep the Sabbath, to observe the Sabbath throughout their generations as a perpetual covenant. It is a sign between Me and the children of Israel forever, for in six days the LORD made the heavens and the earth, and on the seventh day He rested and was refreshed."
Exodus 31:16,17

THE SABBATH MEAL - A WEEKLY SECRET THAT BONDS THE HEBREW PEOPLE TO THE ALMIGHTY AND EACH OTHER

[Location Rawlings home on a Sabbath evening]

To this very day at each Sabbath meal the father in nearly every Jewish home worldwide pronounces the Aaronic blessing over his sons by laying his hands on them in prayer saying, *"May the Lord make you like, <u>Ephraim and Manasseh,</u> may the Lord bless you and keep you; may the Lord make His face to shine upon you and be gracious unto you... may the Lord lift up His face upon you and give you peace.* Numbers 6:24 -26.

Now when my non-Jewish viewers observe a Jewish Sabbath meal they will immediately realize that it is just that; "a feast". This day is set aside on a weekly basis. It is anticipated, and loved by all. The wife and mother carefully plans the food, and prepares it all lovingly, inviting family and friends to come together to rejoice and celebrate the goodness of the God of Israel. It is the highlight of the week, a love feast for everyone involved. That is why two candles are always lit by the mother of the home, with her daughters, before the Sabbath meal begins. The candles represent two witnesses. Of course more than two candles maybe lit.

Why are the names of Joseph's sons, **Ephraim and Manasseh** used in the Shabbat blessing over the male children? After all they were born of his Egyptian wife. Her father was a priest in the pagan Temple of On? The reason is simple. This is a confirmation that wherever the Jewish people migrate over the earth and whoever their mothers are...even those born to non-Jews, their sons are always to remember their Jewish heritage and responsibility to be a *"Light unto the Nations."* Joseph raised his sons with their Jewish identity, and they became two tribes, blessed by their Grandfather Jacob. What a testimony to the millions of Jewish sons living outside of the Land of Israel to this very day. These sons were not assimilated. No doubt, Joseph's wife joined him in faith, for he was blessed with family unity. Then we bless the girl children in the name of our biblical matriarchs.

Also, at every Sabbath meal, each Friday evening, the father of the home blesses his wife, in front of the children, calling her a *"woman of valor"* or in Hebrew an *"eshet chayil."*
The husband reads aloud the blessings from Proverbs 31:10-31. I recommend that every husband read this portion of Scripture to his wife, at least once every week in front of his children. It will do wonders for your marriage no matter what your religious upbringing or affiliation. My wife has chosen to respond to me by reciting Psalm 1, *"blessed is the man..."* this also sends a very positive message to one's children and grandchildren.
It is a feast that also celebrates one's generations as the Lord chose for us to do from the very beginning. We are made aware of how much inter-generational strength and wisdom there is to be shared around the Shabbat table.

The Sabbath feast begins with the Father of the home saying the Kiddush blessing over the wine and the bread. During this prayer of thanksgiving for the Sabbath meal the father also thanks God for "deliverance from Egyptian slavery and bondage. In fact this same prayer is recited at **EVERY JEWISH CEREMONY AND AT EVERY JEWISH CELEBRATION THROUGHOUT THE YEAR!** That's how important it is!

Why is this so? It is because before the first Passover and the deliverance from Egyptian slavery the Jews were then only a "family" or a "clan" or at most a "tribe."

Now, today we as a people and nation, are never allowed to forget that the Lord God of Israel freed us from slavery. He changed times and seasons right in front of the hard hearted wicked, self-absorbed Pharaoh. Our God made a way where there was no way. He gave us miracles before Pharaoh. He showed us the mystery of slaying one of the Egyptian "gods", a lamb, and painting our lentils and door posts with its blood. This act of pure obedience saved our first born sons from the Death Angel. He moved upon nature, parting of the Red (Reed) Sea. He allowed Moses to receive our National Charter or Declaration of Independence known as the Ten Commandments on Mount Sinai.

Then and only then the former families, clans, tribes, and slaves became **"Am Israel"** or the **"Nation of Israel."** This miracle is part and parcel of our daily lives, and existence today. We continue to be threatened on every side. Thus it is vital, that we as a Nation, always remember our gift of "Freedom" at every Jewish celebration.

For us the miracle of miracles of the 20th century was the creation of the modern State of Israel made up of the regathered Jewish people. Starting in the 1880's they were restored to their ancient homeland in waves of immigration. The modern State of Israel, reborn on May 14th 1948, is a huge event in the history of the Jewish people and the world. It is bigger than any one knows or understands. It is perhaps the greatest prophetic sign of this age. The enemies of Israel and the Jewish people also understand very well the significance of this national rebirth while dreading Israel's good success. They work around the clock continually calling for the destruction of Israel. Why? Lets now discuss some reasons why Israel is unique?

"AM ISRAEL" - A UNIQUE NATION AMONG THE NATIONS

Seven Biblical Reasons - WHY?

[Location - Mt of Olives - Jerusalem Israel]

1. Israel is the ONLY NATION promised
   "National Redemption".
   "And who is like Your people, like Israel, the one nation on earth whom God went to redeem for Himself as a people. to make for Himself a name--and to do for Yourself great and awesome deeds, for Your land-- before Your people whom You redeemed for Yourself from Egypt, the nations and their gods? For You have made Your people Israel Your very own people forever; and You Lord, have become their God."
   2 Samuel 7:23-24

2. Israel is the ONLY NATION promised:
   "Everlasting Salvation."
   "But Israel shall be saved by the Lord with an everlasting salvation." Isaiah 45:17

3. Israel is the ONLY NATION threatened: with annihilation and elimination by many other nations continually.
   "Behold Your enemies make a tumult; and those who hate You have lifted up their head. They have taken crafty counsel against Your people and consulted against Your sheltered ones. They have said, 'Come and let us cut them off from being a nation, that the name of Israel be remembered no more.'" Psalm 83:2-4

4. Israel is the ONLY NATION that promises: **to be a blessing to the other nations.**
"I will make you a great nation, I will bless you and make your name great and you shall be a blessing. I will bless those who bless you, and I will curse him who curses you; and in you all the families of the earth will be blessed." *Genesis 12:1-3*

5. Israel is the ONLY NATION that has a continual struggle: **to have it's capital city JERUSALEM, recognized by the other nations.**
"And it shall happen in that day that I will make Jerusalem a very heavy stone for all peoples; all who would heave it away will surely be cut in pieces, though all nations of the earth are gathered against it." Zechariah 12: 3

6. Israel is the ONLY NATION that promises: **to bring PEACE to all the other nations.**
"For unto us a child is born, unto us a Son is given; and the government will be upon His shoulder. And His name will be called Wonderful, Counsellor, Mighty God, Everlasting Father, Prince of PEACE. Of the increase of His government and peace there shall be no end." *Isaiah 9;6,7a*

7. Israel is the ONLY NATION : **to bring the light of The Lord God of Israel and His Messiah to all the nations.**
"I the Lord, have called you in righteousness, and I will hold your hand; I will keep you and give you as a covenant to the people, as a light to the Gentiles or nations." Isaiah 42:6

(Note: this verse, Isaiah 42:6, along with 1 Corinthians 13, were the favorite Bible passages of the first Israeli Prime Minister David Ben Gurion.)

World Systems

- Daniel 2:28-35 interpreted the dream/vision of Nebuchadnezzar's statue - Key to history & future
- Head - God - absolute rulers - Kings
- Chest - Silver - demagogues - Emperors
- Belly - Bronze - despots - Dictators
- Legs - Iron - Democratic rule & money
- Feet - Iron and Clay mixed, Clay = Islam

Israel, the Nations and the Future

Part 4

WORLD SYSTEMS

[Film location - Nebi Musa - Judean Desert Israel]

The Dream and Vision of the Nations Past, Present and Future

Now back to the Hebrew Prophet Daniel. King Nebuchadnezzar's dream reaches from antiquity all the way down in to our world today. The interpretation of it by Daniel is perhaps the most accurate understanding of the past, the present and the future of the nations ever recorded in human history. It was about 600 BCE. All of the spiritual leaders in Babylon were shaking. King Nebuchadnezzar was furious. His chief eunuch alerted the Royal "spiritual advisors" that they were all to be killed if they couldn't tell the King his dream and it's meaning. **Only one - Daniel, the young Hebrew captive**, asked for some more time that he might seek the God of Heaven in prayer, for the answer. See Daniel 2:16

After several days he came back to the king's representative with good news. He said, *"There is a God in heaven who reveals secrets and what will be in the latter days."* Daniel 2: 28 This is a definite reference to the end times, the very days in which we are living. This man Daniel, was one of the most powerful of all Biblical prophets. So now lets examine this dream and vision of the king, according to what the Spirit of God revealed to Daniel as he waited in prayer.

Daniel said confidently, *"The head of gold O King Nebuchadnezzar is you!"* The Babylonian Empire represented the highest authority on earth at that time. "Your rulership" Daniel explained, "is absolute, which can never be questioned."

Next, he said, *"**the chest, shoulder and arms are of silver**"* represent a kingdom slightly less authoritative but still headed by Emperors with absolute power. History shows that the next authority to appear on the earth was the Persian rule - under Darius. Later the Medo-Persian empire appeared, under Cyrus; both men were demagogues. Yet, miraculously Cyrus released the Jews to return to rebuild Jerusalem. Why? It was a fulfillment of Jeremiah's prophecy of a 70 year captivity.

The belly and thighs are of bronze; represents a dictatorial rule such as the Grecian ruler ship under Alexander the Great. However by this time the seeds of democratic ideals had been conceived in the 5th century BCE through Greek philosophers, especially in the Athenian city state where leaders were elected by eligible citizens. But the reality of the excesses of power vested in one person or ruling system still persisted and does so to this present day. If you notice each succeeding metal is worth less in monetary value and is less malleable.

Next came **"the legs of iron"**, which some Bible scholars consider to be a reference to the Roman Empire with their branched system of government. Yes it had serious flaws. It consisted first of, Consuls or the Monarchy. Secondly, the Senate - made up of aristocrats, elders, patricians & plebeians. Thirdly, the Assembly, made up of members of the Army, and all other citizens. The only problem here was that the Emperor was appointed - sometimes for life - like Julius Caesar, as a "god king." Each man was meant to have one vote; which reflects democratic ideals, but in reality the aristocrats or the "elite' ruled. Finally, the vision-dream of Nebuchadnezzar showed the lowest extremities - **"the feet"**.

Next Daniel saw **"the feet of iron, mixed with clay,"** we know that such elements do not melt or merge together. This vision revealed the toes as being brittle. Hence, the feet are a mixture of authorities that do not coalesce; making up very unstable or weak ruling systems exactly as we see in the earth today.

Democracy and Islam will not and cannot ever mix. This is proven every day at the UN and in the "Arab Spring" attempt at democracy from 2010 to the present. The mix is not happening in France, or Britain, or in Europe or the USA or Canada, where problems and struggles are on going between the ruling authorities of democracies and the dictates of Islam.

God opened the mysteries of this mighty statue to Daniel. He understood the final meaning of this profound dream-vision of the heathen king. As he pondered it, Daniel, witnessed *"a stone being cut out of a mountain without hands."* In other words it was a stone of Divine origin and heavenly power that struck the image on it's weakest point - **the feet.** Note: this stone was of humble origin - hard stone, perhaps granite. It was nothing to be compared to the gold, silver, bronze and iron, but it was powerful...***very powerful.***

Daniel watched as this **"stone"** was sent to smash the *"iron and clay feet"* into pieces, causing the entire statue to fall and crumble. All of its parts were reduced to dust before his eyes. Next, **the wind or "the Spirit"**, (*"Ruach"* in Hebrew) scattered and blew away all the useless dust of the image by its gale force until every trace of it had disappeared. So much for the great "World Systems" of government!

Meanwhile,
> *"the stone, grew and grew and grew until it becomes a great mountain that filled the entire earth."* Daniel 2:35

This is a mystery of eternal dimensions. It clearly shows that the **"Ultimate Sovereign"** of history and of human government is **"The Great Creator" - the God of Israel.**
Yes, God alone! Now, lets look at the modern democratic nations on earth today to see how they really function. You may be surprised at what you learn.

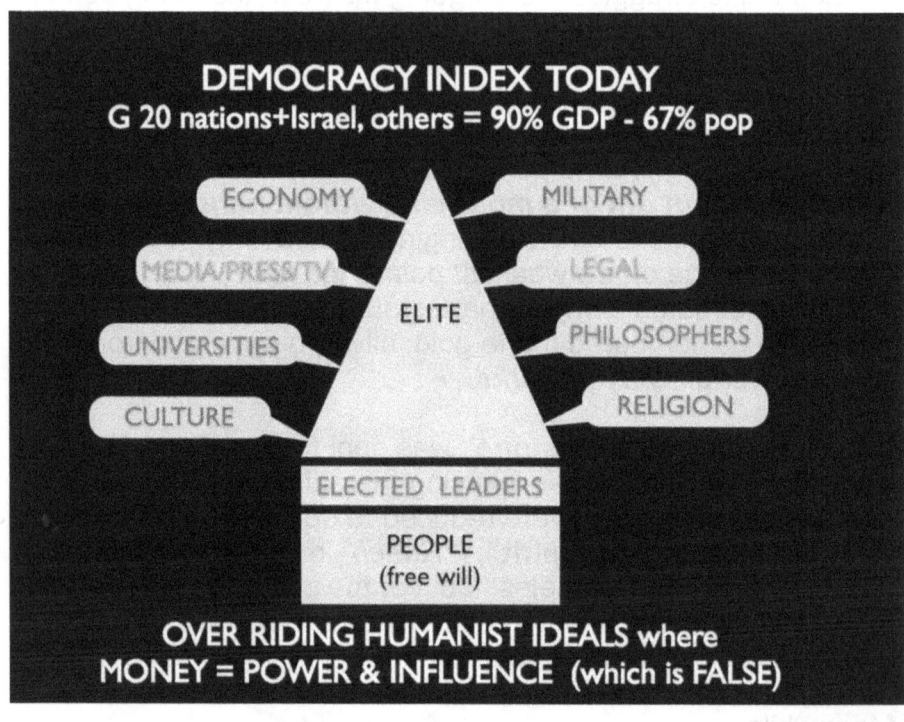

Israel, The Nations and the Future

Part 5

Democracy Today

[Slide #6 - location - Mevasseret Zion, outskirts of Jerusalem]

Now we turn our attention to the most prevelant political system on earth today... democracy.
This slide presents recent findings of Democracy Index compiled by the *Economist Intelligence Unit*, measuring the state of Democracy in 167 countries worldwide, of which 165 are UN Member states.

The Democracy Index, based on 60 indicators, is grouped in 5 different categories such as:
1.   electoral process
2.   Pluralism
3.   civil liberties/human rights
4.   functioning of government
5.   political participation, including political culture.

REGIME TYPES

The Democracy Index categorizes countries as one of four regime types:
1.   full democracies
2.   flawed democracies
3.   hybrid regimes
4.   authoritarian regimes

The overview shows that there are only 25 full democracies in the world today, equalling 15% of the countries. This represents only 11.3% of the world's population. Israel is categorized as a "flawed democracy".

It is also important to note in the Democracy Index report of 2012/2013, that Russia was downgraded from a "hybrid regime" to an "authoritarian regime" due to Vladimir Putin's decision to run again in the 2012 presidential election, with literally no opposition. He became President, once again, by simply switching positions with Dmitry Medvedev, his Prime Minister.

THE ELITE IN DEMOCRATIC SOCIETY

In this slide, I show a two dimensional diagram attempting to portray the multi-dimensional functions of democracy. But it is important to see that in normal democratic conditions the elected representatives are voted into office once every 4 years or so **by the free will of the people.** These elected "Congressmen or Members of Parliament" are "to serve" their citizens by doing the will of the people. That is the ideal. In reality though, most democratic nations are governed on a daily basis by groups of **"elite individuals or experts"** in their fields. Lets start clockwise from the top left of this slide, I am referring here to the "economists and banking officials" such as the Federal Reserve in the USA, who set financial policies for a country. These appointed advisors are not elected officials, but are individuals who wield enormous power over a nation.

The same can be said regarding the defense establishment, better known as 'military experts'. Consider also, the Supreme Court judges who in most democracies are completely autonomous. This is healthy but remember they are <u>not elected</u>. Professors at universities and philosophers have power through their teachings and writings, while movie makers and authors exert enormous influence in society as witnessed by the power of "Hollywood" worldwide. Media experts including press and TV news reporters as well as television executives and writers also have enormous power and influence over social/political issues. Their ideas are ingested by viewers day by day on the "tube".

There are major weaknesses. In the USA, it was discovered that 80% of those who decide on TV content are atheist: while the viewing audience classified themselves to be 80% sympathetic to God! Perhaps this explains why some call their TV, "the idiot box"!!

Such influential people are called the "elite" of society. Yet they are not elected but have a very powerful **daily influence** over their societies. Meanwhile the **elected "leaders" get into office only once every four years and do not have the same degreee of influence as the ELITE**. The conclusion is that elite groups actually rule democratic nations day by day like the "aristocracy" did in antiquity.

Now, here is the bottom line of democracy: THE OVER RIDING IDEALS IN SUCH COUNTRIES PROVE THAT MONEY (the huge funds needed to get elected) CAN AND UNFORTUNATELY OFTEN DO EQUAL POWER AND INFLUENCE WHICH THEN LEADS TO POWER STRUGGLES, CRONYISM AND CORRUPTION. Yet, free will still operates to some degree, even though it is not a fail safe system.

Now, in Part 6, lets consider another kind of government or ruling power that is based on strict religious ideals. I am referring here to Islam.

The meaning of "Islam" in Arabic is "submission"!
According to their dogma, **one's "free will" must be submitted** to **"Shariah or Islamic Law"** which is based on the ideals of Mohammed's teachings as found in the Koran. I call it **"Islam-ocracy"**.

Today, this religious system rules 33% of the earth's population.

ISLAM-OCRACY rules 1/3 of people on earth
Socio - Political - Economic - Religious - System
"Islam means "submission" to Shariah Law - No Free Will
MUST take part in "JIHAD" called "The Project" for Islam to rule all people!

Allah
Koran - Mohammed
Hadiths - Sunni - Shi'ite divide
Muslim messiah - "Mahdi" = 12th imam
Ayatollahs - Iran, Syria, Lebanon = Hezbullah
Moslem Brotherhood in Egypt, plus...
Wahabi's in Saudi Arabia +
Al Qu'eda in Pakistan +

- Refugees
- 45 million
- WMD's

People = "Arab Spring" an attempt at democracy

Islam super imposes, suffocates, eliminates and is intolerant - based on lies. Totalitarian & causes chaos & lawlessness. Produces Terror, Violence and War globally. See Matt 24: 3 - 14

Israel, The Nations and the Future

Part 6

Islam-ocracy

[Slide #7 - location - Mevasseret Zion - suburb of Jerusalem]

This slide is my attempt at showing how "you cannot fit a LARGE round peg in to a SMALL square box". The square box at the bottom shows the recent efforts by some Muslim nations to embrace democracy. Sadly, as we have seen, it is quite a futile exercise.... Why?

FREE WILL versus ISLAMIC SHARIAH LAW

The answer has to do with the **"free will"** of the people. Democracy is meant to safeguard **"the will of the people"** who elect the leaders of their choice. Despots and religious Islamists do not permit this privilege. Of late, autocratic rulers have been disposed in countries such as Egypt, Tunisia, Libya, and Yemen during what has been coined *"The Arab Spring".* This term refers to the noble, "peoples revolution" to remove oppressive leaders from various Mid East nations. Sadly in each place few suitable democratic leaders have yet to be elected or to continue on in office. Why? Because, it seems that the basic philosophy of their opponents always pushes the populations to slip back to their "default system" of authoritarian fundamentalist Islam...submission.

This proves that the ultimate authority in Muslim society tends be in the hands of the religious clerics. They demand that their people submit to Shariah Law and Koranic teachings, which teach 'submission not 'free will'. This is completely opposed to a democratic constitution. So the fledgling aspirants of democracy in each Arab state are up against the odds of militant fundamentalists.

Egypt's fight with the *Muslim Brotherhood* is a perfect example of this dysfunction. Note how quickly Egypt went back to their "default system". This time, Morsi's elected Muslim Brotherhood was replaced by a strong military regime under Generals. Strangely, the latter's rulership leans toward the authoritarian dysfunctional government of deposed former President Hosni Mubarak that lasted for decades. Libya, likewise has yet to emerge with a proper democratic rule after the demise of Muamar Gaddafi.

THE SYRIAN SHAMBLES

"Our authorities have documented the killing of 202,354 Syrian people since March 2011," Syrian Observatory for Human Rights director Rami Abdel Rahman told AFP, adding that more than 130,000 of them were combatants. (January 2015)
It is especially poignant because the basic cause of this war is the age old religious battle between Shi'ite and Sunni Moslems. This same struggle cost over a million young lives in the eight year **Iran - Iraq War in the 1980's.** It was termed, *"The Battle for Jerusalem."* Will this sickness be repeated in Syria? So far no clear solution has emerged. World leaders seem powerless to prevent the horrific on going suffering. Now, to complicate matters, a third front has emerged in the Syrian debacle, and that is, extremist al Qaeda terror factions. No one really knows if and when President Assad is ousted what kind of unpredictable extremist regime may replace him?

PUTINS POSITION IN ALL THIS?

Why does Russia keep backing the cruel, despotic Syrian ruler Bashir al Assad? Clearly, it is for military and strategic purposes that are fueling a new "Cold War" in the world. Vladimir Putin must keep his submarine naval base on the Syrian Mediterranean coastal town of Tarsus. Neither will he give up the Crimean peninsula for similar military reasons. Putin has transformed his old Soviet navy into an ultra modern strike force based on submarine technology and nuclear missile capability.

The quickly developing tensions in the region certainly have Biblical dimensions.

When reading Ezekiel 38, the Bible refers to "Gog, the prince of Rosh" - a power of the north, with a mighty army, who will hatch "an evil plan" to come down "to take a spoil" from "a land of unwalled villages". Could that "booty" be the trillions of cubic feet of natural gas that Israel has discovered and now controls at the eastern end of the Mediterranean Sea? This natural resource seriously challenges Russian hegemony over their supply of natural gas to Europe. With sanctions now being imposed on Russia Putin is getting desperate.
For details, see Ezekiel 38:1-23

REFUGEES AND WMD'S

When one scans the unrest in the world today, much of it can be linked to fundamentalist Muslim terror against Christians, which is creating more martyrs today than ever in the history of the world. Islam is moving stealthily inside the African nations. *The United Nations High Commission on Refugees* (UNHCR) has released the fact that most of the 45 million refugees being created today are the result of Muslim "jihadists". The number of refugees is increasing by 28,000 every day and has become a huge global problem. No one really knows how to deal with this humanitarian issue. I believe this is the moment for Christian families in the West to step up to the plate and start adopting refugees, family by family. Meridel and I are doing it. We have adopted two Christian refugee families from South Sudan. It is not easy, we have to fight the bureaucracy and graft, but we can bring hope to lives of those that are hopeless. What a blessing these folk are because of their steadfast faith in the goodness of God, in spite of man's inhumanity to man!

As I see it, Muslim rulers will never give up their aspirations to control "weapons of mass destruction" in their struggle to rule the world by Shari'ah Law. This "holy war" against the "infidels" or Israelis, Jews, and Christians is now termed by Islam, **"The Project".** This plan is to give Islam more "respectability".

What a sad joke! Islamic fundamentalists have set their sights on Europe and are moving steadily toward making it "Eurabia" in the next decade. The frightening thing is that they are making progress. They do it very subtly using local democratic electoral systems and demographics. They elect Muslims into office. Then the high Muslim birth rate means that the Western nations will be taken over by their Muslim minorities in a few years via the "weapon of the womb" as it was termed by Yasser Arafat. Islam-ocracy bent on take over the 'West' is fueled by zealots operating in largely "dozing or comatose" Western nations. The situation seems hopeless, but is it...? The Holy One of Israel is not sleeping and neither is Israel!

Now lets move to the next slide, to see a governing system called "Theocracy" - better known as **the government that will never end!!!!** For details, see Isaiah 9:7

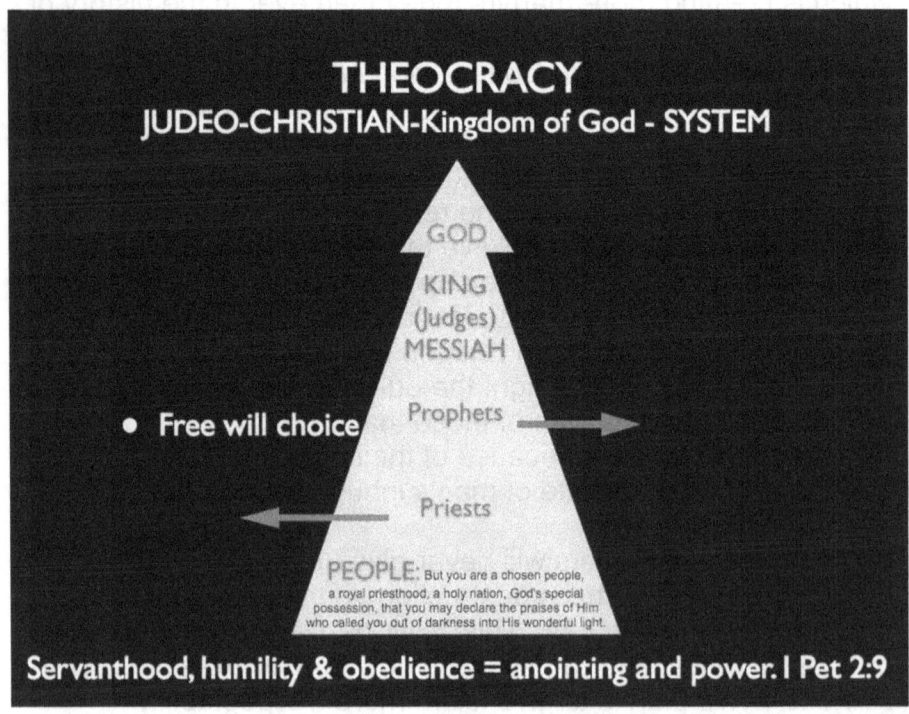

Israel, The Nations and the Future

Part 7

Theocracy

[Slide #8 location - Mevasseret Zion - Suburb of Jerusalem]

Recognizing Authorities

The hallmark of Theocracy is its basic principle of recognizing God, the Lord Almighty to be the **"Supreme Authority"** over everything and everybody on earth - now and forever. In this form of government, the King of Kings, the Messiah, represents our unseen "Heavenly Father", known as the "King of the Universe".

Nearly every Jewish prayer starts of with ***"Baruch Ata Adoni, Elohenu, Melech ha Olam"* which means "Blessed are You O Lord, our God, <u>King</u> of the Universe".** So the Kingdom of God is an essential part of Jewish thought and understanding.

One day the Kingdom of God will be acknowledged by everyone on earth as the final ruling authority. Meanwhile this Kingdom exists in the hearts of God's people worldwide; albeit unseen. The reality of this invisible Kingdom is powerfully and clearly sensed and felt by believers, Jewish and Christian and sincere seekers of any nation or background alike...everywhere,

When we founded the *International Christian Embassy Jerusalem* in September 1980. I was the Media Director the day the "Embassy" opened. Mayor Teddy Kollek cut the gold ribbon and said, *"In my long career as Mayor of this city I have opened many important buildings, but this one is the most important one of all."*

Why did he say this? He was not a religious man, but he was "spiritual". He could "see" with the eyes of God's Spirit, the significance of opening this small apartment that represented an 'Embassy, giving a voice in Jerusalem' for Christians all around the world. He saw them as part of the Kingdom of God on earth that would in the future, strongly stand with Israel in her historic and Biblical cause.

In fact, after the ribbon cutting ceremony many people were milling around and soon I was surrounded by a group of Israelis. In typical fashion they queried me with some tough questions: "This is a nice thing you have done today, but every Embassy represents a country. Which country do you represent?"
With out hesitation, I replied, "We don't just represent a country but we represent a 'Kingdom on earth'."
"Oh, yes, yes of course." They seemed truly respectful, nodding and smiling in approval. Immediately they grasped the true meaning of this event.

FREE WILL CHOICE GUARANTEED

The other essential principle of Theocracy is its commitment to safe guarding the "free will choice" of its adherents. The King, the Messiah is the King of Kings on earth and no one in this Kingdom is forced to serve Him. By observing the character qualities of servanthood, humility and obedience, first exemplified by the King of Love; one can grow in grace by embracing this King. Those same characteristics grow in each one as they choose to serve in various capacities.

For example: the Prophets represent God to man and speak His Word in due season. While Priests or intercessors speak to God on behalf of man making their requests or appeals known to the Supreme Court of Courts. This is known as prayer!So the people have their representatives though they are not elected per se.

By virtue of submitting to this Highest Authority and willingly serving, each one receives their tasks and carry them out with the enabling anointing or presence of the Holy Spirit. Here are examples as found in the Bible.

> *"But you are a chosen people, a royal priesthood, a holy nation, God's special possession, that you may declare the praises of Him who called you out of darkness into His wonderful light."* 1 Peter 2:9

> *"Now, therefore, if you will indeed obey my voice and keep my covenant, then you shall be a special treasure to Me above all people; for all the earth is Mine. 'And you shall be to Me a kingdom of priests and a holy nation'. These are the words which you (Moses) shall speak to the children of Israel."* Exodus 19: 5,6

The Kingdom of God on Earth!

- Daniel understood the vision *"where a stone was cut without hands which struck the image on its feet of iron (democracy) and clay (Islam) and broke them in pieces... and the stone became a great mountain (the Kingdom of God) and it filled the whole earth."* Daniel 2:34 and 35b; Isaiah 9:6,7

- Jesus said that false messiahs and lawlessness would abound, but we are to endure to the end and to preach the gospel in all the world... to all nations... then the end will come! Matthew 24:3-14

- Jesus taught that the nations would be divided either as sheep or goats based on how they treated the *"least of My brethren."* Matthew 25:31-40

- Jesus said many times to *"watch and pray!"* Matthew 24:42; 25:13

- *"Pray for the peace of Jerusalem, they shall prosper..."* Psalm 122:6

- Pray for us at *Israel Vision* to keeps sending out the "good news" from Zion.

Israel, The Nations and the Future

Part 8

Kingdom of God on Earth

Now, we go back to the Prophet Daniel, (see above slide) and the amazing understanding that God gave to him concerning the utter and complete collapse of the humanly created, "World Systems". I repeat this here for emphasis. The end of man-made ruling systems is accomplished by **"a stone"**, which *"was cut - without hands - from a mountain. Then it struck the image on it's feet of iron (democracy) and clay (Islam) and broke them in pieces."* Daniel 2:34

I believe this "**stone**" is a clear reference to the Messiah. The Psalmist says,
The stone which the builders rejected has become the chief cornerstone. Psalm 118:22

"Then Daniel saw how this "stone" became a great mountain that filled the whole earth, while the feet and the rest of the parts of the image became dust that the wind blew away until nothing remained. Meanwhile the stone grows and grows and eventually fills the whole earth." Daniel 2:35

To me this mountain is a direct reference to the **growth of the Kingdom of God on earth, while the wind is a reference to the Spirit of God** that completely removes every vestige of the dust of the old, natural, man made, "World Systems" on earth.

Closing Prayer - with Audience Participation

- Pray for your nation, for government leaders, for pastors and cell groups and house groups for Israel.
- Pray for Israel - protection from terror, violence, war and WMD's. Protection from deception - False Peace
- Pray for your church and its leaders
- Pray for believers in Israel + *Israel Vision*
- Pray for revival everywhere in the hard times ahead and pray for the *"Peace of Jerusalem"*
- Pray for Syria, Iraq, Iran, other Muslim nations! Revival!

You, my dear reader are a part of this victorious Kingdom that will have no end if you simply ask to be "Born from Above" by the Spirit of God. Do it today. John 3:1-16

May God bless you and yours.

Now lets go on to Part 9 for your participation.

Israel, The Nations and the Future

Part 9

PRAYER - THE GREATEST POWER OF ALL

Now we come to the moment where you get to take part. It is now time for you to engage *your will*. Yes, *your free will*. This is why you were created. You are invited to bring the influence and power of the Kingdom of Heaven, "from above" onto the earth. It is the "unseen" having final influence on the "seen". Let us always remember that the greatest power on earth today is **Prayer** and it is connected directly to the Kingdom of God. I call it the ***Nuclear Power of Prayer***. *It is a Heavenly Power* and there are **Keys** for you to use in this prayer battle. Here is what the Shepherd King says about these **"KEYS"**.

> *"And I will give you the keys of the kingdom of heaven, and whatever you bind (in prayer) on earth will be bound in heaven and whatever you loose (in prayer) on earth will be loosed in heaven".* Matthew 16:19
>
> *"...if two of you agree (in prayer) on earth concerning anything that they ask it will be done for them by My Father in heaven."* Matthew 18:19
>
> *"For where two or three are gathered (to pray) together in My name, I am there in the midst of them".* Matthew 18:20

The Apostle Paul, like the Prophet Daniel, teaches us that our prayer warfare is first in the "unseen realm" and yet it is mighty and powerful:

"For we do not wrestle against flesh and blood, but against principalities, against powers, against the rulers of the darkness of this age, against spiritual hosts of wickedness in heavenly places". Ephesians 6:12

One of our most important tasks in life is "to see and to engage" in the on going battle between human and social "government problems" and how they are affected by the real source of these problems; <u>the dark unseen realm.</u> Without this discernment we end up "wrestling" with "flesh and blood" instead of prayerfully warring against the invisible works of "hell" behind the scenes. The "rulers of darkness" have assignments, and that is to make all people slaves, hopeless, helpless, addicted, depressed and despondent.

But this phrase, **"heavenly places"** points to the mighty resources available to any sincere person of prayer. Take up your eternal destiny right now. Be the prayer warrior that your Heavenly Father intends you to be. He is seeking out "intercessors" everywhere.

> Why can I say this? Because in Ezekiel's time, the Lord said, "...***I sought for a man to stand in the gap and make up the hedge....but I found none"!*** Ezekiel 22:30

Today, thank God this is not the case, - there are now multitudes of serious prayer warriors all over the world and because of them... or should I say...**you...**
- the **Gap** is being filled with God's mercy to meet man's need.
- a protective **Hedge** is being built, around our families, communities and nations, and
- the **Breach** of loneliness and separation between God and man is being repaired daily by our **PRAYERS.**

This is **YOUR** work, the humble person who stands "before God on behalf of others."

As a result of those who are dedicated to *"watch and pray"*...
YOU will,
- <u>bind</u> the ancient/modern 'prince of Persia' spirit over Iran today.
- <u>bind</u> the cruel militaristic/ terror ISIS spirit over Syria and the Middle East today.
- <u>bind</u> the anarchistic, lawless, unbelieving spirit over all the nations today.
- <u>bind</u> the spirit of bondage/submission and enticement to radical Islam.
- <u>loose</u> or use the gift of your "free will" in the power of prayer right into the heart of God. Do it today and the Spirit of God will bless you with the authority to release (loose) the power of our King of Kings - Messiah and the Holy Spirit to bring victory over evil, everywhere in His Name!

It is up to those of us to take the words of Jesus seriously, to pray and believe so that our own **nations will become each one, a "sheep nation"**.

Can you say Amen to that?

CONCLUSION

So what is going to happen in the future when the King of Kings is ruling from His throne in Jerusalem?
Then it is clear from the Word of God that...
- Jerusalem becomes a *"House of Prayer <u>for All Nations</u>"*
- *Peace, Equity and Justice will reign for all people on earth... Amen and Amen!*

Here is how the Prophet Micah beautifully expresses it:

"Now <u>it shall come to pass in the latter days,</u> that the mountain of the Lord's House shall be established on the mountains, and shall be exalted above the hills; and peoples shall flow to it.

<u>*Many nations, shall come and say,*</u> *"Come, and let us go up to the mountain of the Lord, to the house of the God of Jacob; He will teach us His ways, and we shall walk in His paths.' For out of Zion, the law-teachings shall go forth and the word of the Lord from Jerusalem.*

He shall judge between many peoples, and rebuke strong nations afar off; they shall beat their swords into plough shares, and their spears into pruning hooks.
<u>*Nation shall not lift up sword against nation, neither shall they learn war anymore.*</u>

But everyone shall sit under his vine and under his fig tree, and no one shall make them afraid; for the mouth of the Lord of Hosts has spoken it.

For all people walk each in the name of his god, <u>but we will walk in the Name of the Lord our God forever and ever.</u>'"

Micah 4: 1-5

Part 10 - Your Part

[Narrator]
The producer of these programs - Jerusalem Vistas - Israel Vision is a "faith based charitable organization". We depend on viewer and reader participation to continue the work of publishing the Good News among the Nations from Israel.

For 45 years now, by God's grace, we have produced 1000's of inspirational, Bible based teachings on film & TV, including 140 documentaries, and 100's of "talk shows" in Jerusalem.

The Founders/Directors encourage you to be apart of the team and to contribute to the Blog via the Internet. We invite you to join us and share the information with your friends far and wide. Please go to:

israelvisiontv.blogspot.co.il

Jerusalem Vistas - Israel Vision

Team Members give lectures, and power points on many aspects of history, current events, the Bible and life inside of Israel today. They are available for *Family Healing Seminars* and other special presentations on Israel. Jay and Meridel's books and booklets, DVD's CD's, Mp3's and other audio-visual presentations such as Keynote and Power Points are available for you to use in your home, church or prayer cell.

But we can't do it alone!

We are very grateful to our partners, who enable us to continue this vital work.

Suggested ways you may Participate:

To make a donation - go to our blog where you can donate using any major credit card, via,
1. PayPal - see - israelvisiontv.blogspot.co.il, use the "donate" button, or
2. Send cheques made out to *"Jerusalem Vistas"* to the address below. Please note: post dated cheques are very helpful, or
3. Email us your credit card details. Be sure to include,
- Name, as it appears on your card
- Full address,
- Credit card number and type
- Expiry date,
- Amount of gift, and
- One time or monthly

We will send you a receipt by post.

Please note: For your gifts to Jerusalem Vistas - Tax Deductible Receipts are available in USA, Canada, UK, Germany, and Israel.

4. Thanks for praying and may God bless you and yours.

About the Speakers/Authors

Drs Jay and Meridel Rawlings are dual citizens of Canada and Israel. Israel has been their focus since 1969 when they launched out from Jerusalem to visit Jewish communities world wide over several decades. Their first book Fishers and Hunters details some of these incredible encounters. Israel Vision Studios were founded in 1980 through which Jay has written, produced and directed some 140 documentaries of various aspects of life in Israel, educating a global audience. This unique film library records on video key events covering over half of the modern history of the reborn State of Israel. They were also part of the founders of the International Christian Embassy in Jerusalem.

Israel Vision their weekly TV show www.israelvision.tv gives a Biblical perspective on Israel's historic cause. Their daily blog www.israelvision.tv/blogspot.com keeps a keen Internet audience informed from Jerusalem on current affairs and issues for prayer.

Dr. Meridel Rawlings is a researcher, writer, speaker, TV hostess, and therapist for the sexually abused. www.stillsmallvoice.tv

The Rawlings' four sons are actively involved in the ongoing work.

CONTACT INFO

**Drs Jay and Meridel Rawlings
founders / directors
Jerusalem Vistas/ Israel Vision**

PO Box 40101
Mevasseret Zion, 91400, Israel

Email: jvrawlings@gmail.com

Fax: +972 2 534 1271

Tel: +972 2 533 0382 during Israel office hours
(otherwise leave your message and number for call-back)

Production Stills

by C. Stephan

David Rawlings filming the Western Wall (Kotel)

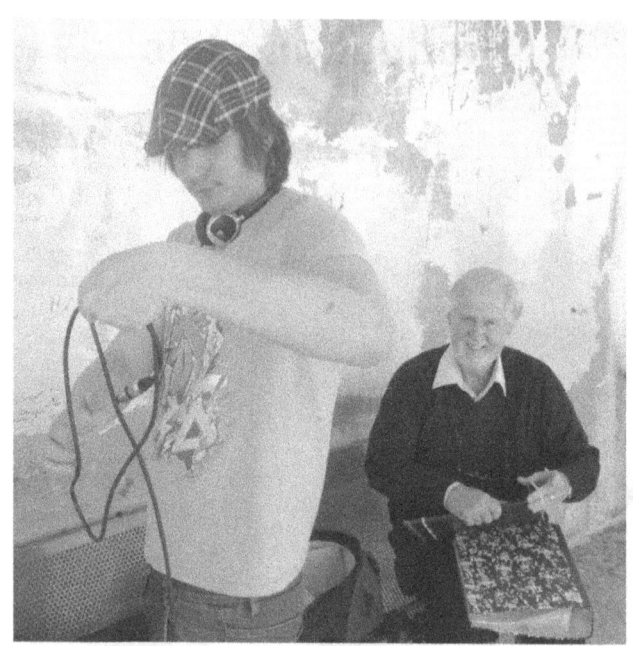

Daniel Rawlings and Jay Rawlings preparing to film near the Western Wall in Jerusalem

Daniel Rawlings, our cameraman, near Nebi Musa

David Rawlings, our producer, out in the Judean Desert near Nebi Musa

Notes

Notes

www.ingramcontent.com/pod-product-compliance
Lightning Source LLC
Chambersburg PA
CBHW061511040426
42450CB00008B/1560